WHY ARE THERE DIFFERENT COMPUTER LANGUAGES?

Kirsty Holmes

COMPUTERS AND <CODING>

KidHaven
PUBLISHING

Published in 2019 by KidHaven Publishing, an Imprint of Greenhaven Publishing, LLC
353 3rd Avenue, Suite 255, New York, NY 10010

© 2019 Booklife Publishing

This edition is published by arrangement with Booklife Publishing.

Written by: Kirsty Holmes
Edited by: Holly Duhig
Designed by: Danielle Jones

Cataloging-in-Publication Data

Names: Holmes, Kirsty.
Title: Why are there different computer languages? / Kirsty Holmes.
Description: New York : KidHaven Publishing, 2019. | Series: Computers and coding | Includes glossary and index.
Identifiers: ISBN 9781534527249 (pbk.) | ISBN 9781534527232 (library bound) | ISBN 9781534527256 (6 pack)
Subjects: LCSH: Programming languages (Electronic computers)--Juvenile literature. | Computer programming--Juvenile literature.
Classification: LCC QA76.7 H645 2019 | DDC 005.26′2--dc23

IMAGE CREDITS

Cover – izabel.l, I000s_pixels, Macrovector, danjazzia. 5 – hanss. 6 – Sudowoodo. 7 – Macrovector, OmniArt. 8 – Pogorelova Olga, Maksim M, 32 pixels, Dacian G. 9 – mamanamsai, Faith Nyky. 10 – Sudowoodo, Kit8.net, Hasik-ioj, SofiaV. 11 – Jane Kelly. 12 – Sudowoodo. 13 – Sudowoodo, filip robert. 14-15 – Succo Design, Scratch is developed by the Lifelong Kindergarten Group at the MIT Media Lab. See http://scratch.mit.edu. 16 – denk creative, A_KUDR, Sudowoodo. 17 – Top Vector Studio. 18-19 – Shai_Halud. 20-21 – MilkyM. 22 – Igogosha, RinArte, Inspiring. 23 – Oxanne, Sudowoodo.

Printed in the United States of America

CPSIA compliance information: Batch #BS18KL: For further information contact Greenhaven Publishing LLC, New York, New York at 1-844-317-7404.

WHY ARE THERE DIFFERENT COMPUTER LANGUAGES?

COMPUTERS AND <CODING>

PAGE 4	What Is a Computer?
PAGE 6	What Is a Computer Language?
PAGE 8	High- and Low–Level Languages
PAGE 10	Why Are There Different Languages?
PAGE 12	Choosing a Language
PAGE 14	Scratch
PAGE 18	HTML
PAGE 20	Python
PAGE 22	The Internet of Things
PAGE 24	Glossary and Index

Words that look like **this** can be found in the glossary on page 24.

WHAT IS A
COMPUTER?

A computer is a machine **designed** to do a specific job. People can give instructions to a computer to tell it what to do.

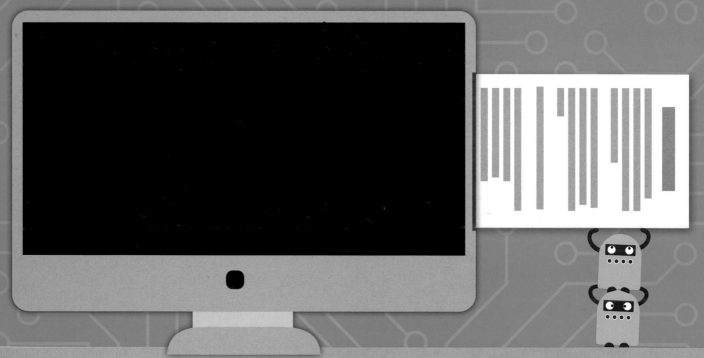

Computers can help us do lots of things very fast, and they don't need to sleep or take breaks. They are very useful!

A set of instructions for a computer is called a program. The instructions themselves are called algorithms and these are written in **languages** called code.

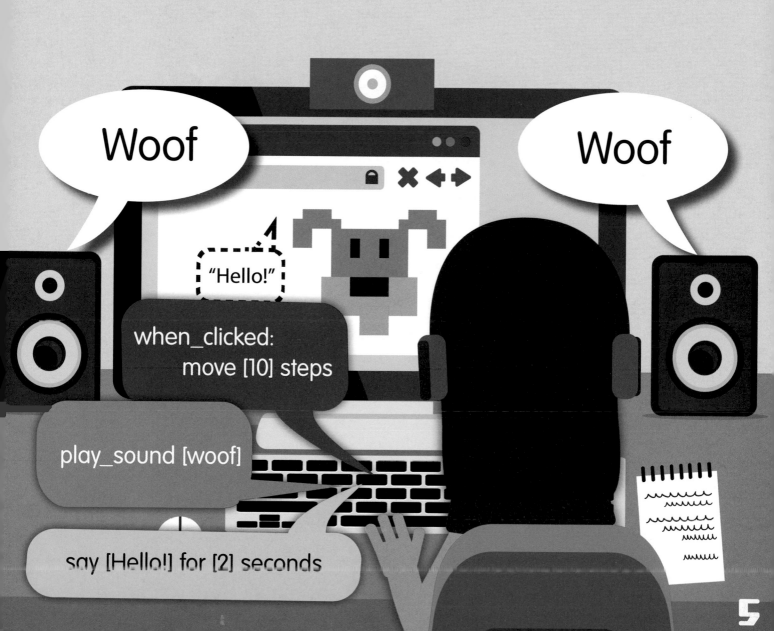

WHAT IS A COMPUTER LANGUAGE?

Humans don't all speak one language – we talk to each other in lots of different languages. Some people can understand many languages.

Bonjour

Nǐ hǎo

DID YOU KNOW?
Changing a word from one language to another is called translating.

Computers can't understand human languages. We tell computers what to do using little **pulses** of electricity. A computer understands that a little pulse means "1" and a gap between two pulses means "0." This is called binary code.

A computer is very smart and can read a long string of 0s and 1s really quickly.

HIGH- AND LOW-LEVEL LANGUAGES

Humans can't really understand binary code. It's too long and boring, and we are much slower than computers. So, to talk to a computer and tell it what to do, we need to translate human language into binary code using a program called a compiler.

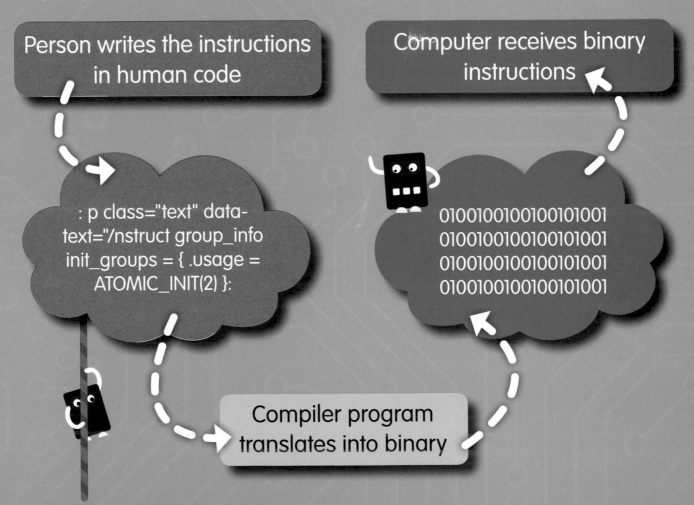

Person writes the instructions in human code

Computer receives binary instructions

: p class="text" data-text="/nstruct group_info init_groups = { .usage = ATOMIC_INIT(2) }:

010010010010101001
010010010010101001
010010010010101001
010010010010101001

Compiler program translates into binary

Binary code is known as a low-level language and the languages people use to code are called high-level languages. Just like humans have different languages for talking to each other, we have lots of languages for talking to computers, too.

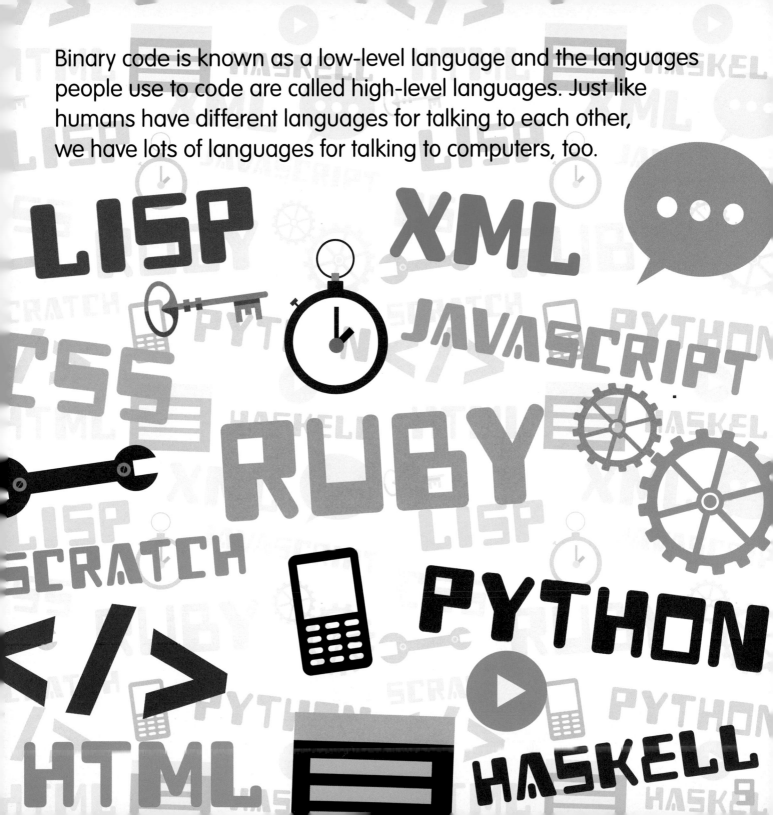

WHY ARE THERE DIFFERENT LANGUAGES?

Sometimes, **similar** things do similar jobs, but they do it in different ways. For example, a bike, truck, and racing car are all **vehicles**, but we choose different vehicles for different jobs.

You wouldn't want to carry all this stuff on a bike!

In the same way, all computer languages are good at different things. Some languages, like JavaScript, are good for the **Internet**. Others are better at telling simple machines what to do.

```
"intelliSenseMode": "msvc-x64",
"browse": {
    "path": [
        "${workspaceRoot}",
        "C:\\MinGW\\lib\\gcc\\mingw32\\6.3.0\\include\\c++"
```

```
document.getElementById("demo").style.fontSize = "25px";
document.getElementById("demo").style.color = "blue";
document.getElementById("demo").style.display = "photo";
```

CHOOSING A LANGUAGE

How do programmers decide which language to use? You might decide to choose a language that everyone you are working with understands.

Some languages use more math, and others use more words. You might choose the one you find easier. It's important to choose the right tool for the job.

SCRATCH

Scratch is a computer language that is used to teach children how to code. It uses colored building blocks to represent instructions and you can build them into algorithms, or formulas. You can make animations and games using Scratch.

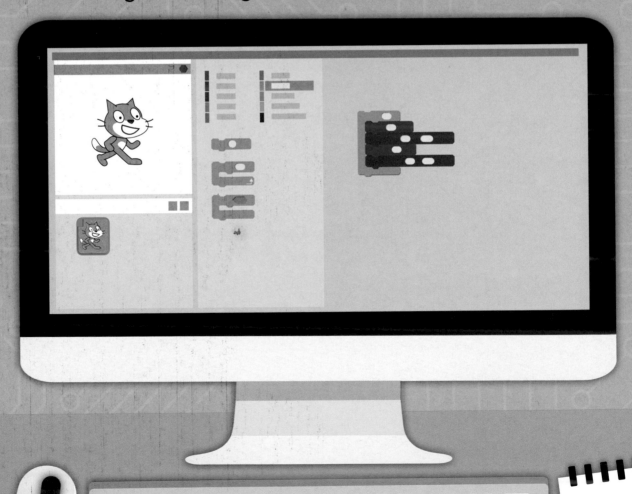

Here, a Scratch program makes the picture of a cat say "Hello!"

Scratch is good for beginners. You can build algorithms easily, look at what other people have made, or change other people's programs to see how they work.

If you visit Scratch online, you can try it for yourself.
Could you make a game? How about a program that
will do your homework for you?

HTML

HTML is a computer language designed to tell computers exactly what you want a website to look like. HTML allows you to design a **webpage** using tags.

Tags are words written inside angle brackets, like this: <p>Hello!<p>

HTML lets you show text and images and decide how the webpage should look.

For example, this piece of coding will show the word "Hello!" in red:
`<font color="red">Hello!</font>`

PYTHON

Python is an **advanced** programming language. Where HTML can only show exactly what you tell it, like drawing in a notepad, Python can use algorithms to process the information you give it and make decisions.

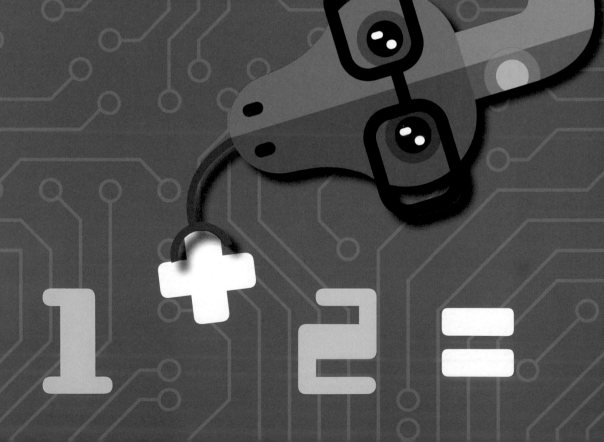

For example, HTML cannot add two numbers together for you, but Python can.

Here, Python is working out what 1 + 2 is and **printing** the answer.

```
> answer = 1 + 2; print(answer)
3
```

THE INTERNET OF THINGS

Computer engineers think that, one day, lots of things will have computers in them, and they will all talk to one another. For example, your freezer would know when you have run out of ice cream and could talk to your computer, telling it to add more to your shopping list.

Your alarm clock could tell your toaster that you were awake, and to start making your toast exactly how you like it. This would save people lots of time… but all our **devices** would need to use the same computer language to talk to each other. Maybe there are new computer languages waiting to be written…

GLOSSARY

ADVANCED far ahead in development and better than most others of its kind

DESIGNED planned for a specific purpose

DEVICES objects designed for a particular purpose, usually machines

INTERNET the world's largest computer network

LANGUAGES system of spoken or written words used for communication

PRINTING (in Python) displaying on a computer screen

PULSES short bursts of a signal

SIMILAR alike; almost the same

VEHICLES machines used for transportation

WEBPAGE a particular part of a website

INDEX

algorithms 5, 14, 16, 20

beginners 16

binary code 7–9

compiler 8

computers 4–5, 7–9, 11, 14, 18, 22–23

Internet of Things 22–23

math 13

programs 5, 8, 15–17

tags 18

tools 13

translating 6, 8

websites 18

working 12, 16, 21